A
NEW
TENANCY

GERARD SMYTH

The Dedalus Press
24 The Heath ~ Cypress Downs ~ Dublin 6W
Ireland

ISBN 1 904556 27 2 (paper)
ISBN 1 904556 28 0 (bound)

Acknowledgements are due to the editors of the following publi-
cations where a number of these poems first appeared: *Agenda,
Cork Literary Review, Irish Pages, The Irish Times, Leviathan
Quarterly, Poetry Ireland Review, The Shop, Southword*. Also,
some of the poems were first published, in English and Roma-
nian, in *Convorbiri Literare* and *The Anthology of the Interna-
tional Poetry Festival of Curtea de Arges*. The version of Montale's
'Syria' was made for *Corno inglese. An Anthology of Eugenio
Montale's Poetry in English Translation* (edited by Marco Sonzogni
and to be published by the Foundation for Italian Studies of
University College Dublin).

Dedalus Press books are represented and distributed in the
U.S.A. and Canada by **Dufour Editions Ltd.**, P.O. Box 7,
Chester Springs, Pennsylvania 19425
in the UK by **Central Books**, 99 Wallis Road, London E9 5LN

The Dedalus Press receives financial assistance from
An Chomhairle Ealaíon, The Arts Council, Ireland.
Printed in Dublin by Johnswood Press

for Pauline

CONTENTS

ONE

THE SOLITARY LIFE

I entered there
as if entering the Temple of Solomon
or a Tibetan monastery of silent prayer.

I hid there, not once but often
passing a morning
in the pantheon of rhetoric
or an evening in spring
turning the pages that carried a tale
of crime and punishment, war and peace.
It was Emily's Amherst,
Homer's Ithaca.

On the reading table,
like a great inheritance,
the books that a match could burn
and turn to embers
were crammed with fictions,
crammed with fables,
crammed with the labours of the solitary life

FINGER-WRITING ON WINDOW DUST
for Diarmaid Ó Muirithe

It's not that long ago
since the bell in the corridor
woke Andromeda,
and the tuning fork tapped on the table
made a sound that melted away.

In the school with ten tall rooms
I was caught once
finger-writing on window dust.
I sat with my slate and abacus
learning to fathom words,
listening to how the world was made.

The sibilance of Gaelic had a power of its own.
Ciúnas settled us down
during the story of Moses
when Moses was found
in the basket of rushes.

A map of Africa showed us
where our pennies were going.
Out in the yard
it was knucklebone to knucklebone.

AFTER MANY YEARS

After many years I pass the house
where I was born.
A house of keepsakes kept in drawers.

The roof is gone, the floors ready to fall.
In the Stygian hall there is only the after-stillness
of the last tenant to leave.

It is nineteen fifty-nine.
The landlord climbs three flights of stairs
to collect the landlord's rent.

My father at the window,
half-erased by dusk, reads his evening paper
or *The Guns of Navarone*.

He sits until it is time to comb
his hair and step into the street
with his hat and coat and ironed handkerchief.

TK's Territory

Beyond Swift's Hospital
and the grey slab wall,
down the lane where you remember
Paul Henry cottages,
it's all breeze-block and brick,
electric gates and double windows.

But this was once a sward
of city vegetation: blackberry fields
where you picked your way
through a rivery smell
and the smell of clay
shared with gull and pigeon.

Beyond Swift's hospital,
in the hollow glade
on the hillpath like a pilgrim's walk,
it was late September,
summer's cadenza of final warmth.
There was shunting

in the distance: the evening train,
the departure whistle.
The hopstore harboured bitter grain.
In the cooperage a craft was dying
there among planks of wood,
hoops of iron.

SAM'S JUNKSHOP

for Peter Keating

In the tenebrous junkshop
he built a shrine to things tossed away.
A display of dross: the strange,
the familiar: mouth organ, jew's harp.

Like a character out of Isaac Bashevis Singer
he stood in the doorway,
his bulk blocking the entrance to the muddle
of disowned and unwanted possessions.

Copper and brass but mostly the poorer metals
of birdcages, clocks and kettles.
Keys no-one needed, a bugle brought back
from the French Foreign Legion.

PORTOBELLO BRIDGE

Twice a day I carry my soul over water.
The seedy canal blackened by car exhaust.
When first I came to the footbridge
at the lock, as a child
with fishing net and pinkeen pot,
it was through Little Jerusalem:
the avenues of exile,
past the synagogue that is now the mosque.

On the long road with dome
and campanile, steps to the doors
and life above the shops,
the town clock faces four ways at once,
chimneys sprout weeds
and windows reveal
lodging-rooms with lanterns
of papier-mâché.

Twice a day I cross the bridge
at Portobello, look to the hills
or leave them behind
in their morning glory beyond Rathmines.

MOUNT ARGUS

The road forks there where a Celtic Cross
was raised in memory of martyrs shot
in a War of Independence.
Two directions: which one to take?
You always knew and always went
through the palisade of Scots pine
into the shadow of Mount Argus.

Your Santiago where you felt anointed
and walked the stations
from *The Betrayal in the Garden*
to *The Hammering of the Nails*.
I was five or six and led by the hand
to the Christmas animals,
the ox and the lamb.

It was like a gloaming in the candlesmoke.
A world between the worlds
of light and dark.
Nothing stirred except the two of us:
a pair of shadows creaking
in quietness that hung there
like the mummy-cloth of Passion Week.

TERRA COGNITA

In the shadow of the woodyard,
in the shelter of the childhood house
I heard the sounds of all the days:
sawblades, factory horn,
song of the delivery-man
who sometimes was
the neighbourhood's Good Samaritan.

The city then was a place of missing pieces,
gaps in the architecture,
generations falling faster than history.
The river — malodorous — ran its course
between the Four Courts
and the Franciscan chapel,
along the route they took
herding cattle to the North Wall
over ground that covered
memento mori, Norse-age dust,
street by street through streets that looked
beaten up, stripped bare.

MID-CENTURY SUNDAY

In those days soon after mid-century
the dead air of Sunday was like a sedative.
It settled on the Dublin Mountains
and Garden of Remembrance.

The radio was a choice
between Dixieland, plainchant
or the shipping forecast told in snatches.
It was the day of darkest moods,
of rain as black as the Sunday prayerbook
and streets all silent

except for the marching band
whose tunes I loved
as much as their walk of righteousness:
the swagger in the way
the musicians advanced,
playing their anthem without looking back.

THE DAYS OF ELVIS

Old friend from evenings
of an age that passed,
the days of Elvis,
today I saw you out on the street,
solemn-looking,
like a man who abandoned
his house and money.

In the dusky air
you were gone in a hurry,
into the distance, untraceable
like a magician's assistant.
It has been decades
since our backstreet shuffle,
our daily colloquy, walking home
with riches in our satchels:
Keats's odes, Cicero's rolling Latin.
The four o'clock saunter
on the way from school,
by walls that seemed to ooze
the ambrosial stench of the brewery.

I remember this: your fingers tapped
to a tune of the time.
Ride a white swan.
That summer's indelible song.

SMOKEHOUSE

The remembered day is over and it has left
the aroma of smoke in your closed house
and something else: the absolute stillness
of empty chairs and iron beds.

One room is laden with clothing
from decades you could never let go of:
winter coats, summer dresses.
Pockets smelling of pinecones and hen-feathers.

The fire that burned through summers past
has petered out, gone to ash.
Soot has settled on the dresser's hanging cups
and glazed mosaic of plates and jugs.

Hallowed with age, everything remains in place:
drawers and boxes stashed with clutter,
the small window of wonder
that frames the good light and the wintry dark.

THE BLACK KETTLE SINGING

According to the custom of the house
I stopped at the threshold and called out
before entering the den with its peatsmoke
and smell of newly-split wood.

The fireside matriarch: old-timer, forbear
tapping her stick on the stone floor,
told me all she knew by heart,
all she could remember

while I said little or nothing at all.
Her hands like fossils were raw from the drill
of pulling cabbage stalks
or knocking clay from potato skin.

In the half-light, in her corner
she had all the room she needed
holding court or dazed by sleep.
Close enough to hear the black kettle singing.

In the Noonday Yard

Two willow trees with towering peaks
stand with aged roots deep in the earth.
A zinc bucket rattles the wind.
And billowing like a length of silk
a nettlebed crowns the golden dungheap.

It seems strange to stand again
in the milking-shed with the empty manger,
dusting down the haymaker's
ball of twine, a whetstone half-erased

and the scythe still sharp. Nothing stirs
but the treetops brimming with heaven's breeze.
Rain in the rain-barrel evaporates
under the eaves in the noonday yard.

KNIFEGRINDER

Once every summer he came,
the knife-sharpener
encumbered with all the tools of his trade:
the whetstone like a stiff tongue,
the grinding-wheel to ignite sparks on the blade.

From over the railway line,
he came to practice his craft
in grandmother's yard. First he'd spit
into the vessel his cupped hands made,
then rub them together,

a kind of ritual gesture
before he honed the metals
of the sickle, the scythe, the cudgel;
made them unsafe to touch and ready as ever
to level the hay-patch down to the stubble,
the last vestige of summer.

Heirloom

Among family heirlooms
I find a postcard written on a voyage
to America: the barely legible last goodbye
of a steamship emigrant.

I imagine him, my ancestor
on the journey west: homesick, heartstruck.
Like a fledgling thrown from the nest
to take a chance
under Liberty's outstretched hand.

I imagine him, sad to leave his bogbanks,
grassland, the sound of the latch,
but ready to seek with rolled-up sleeves
the better life in Queens, the Bronx,
streets with their entourage,
streets that spawned hard tasks.

ARCADIA

Look, the green pastures of Arcadia.
The one-street town, the age-old hill.
In the solstice chamber
light is visible only for a while.
Christmas frost is silvering
the cycle ways, the birch wood
and the railway line.

Here in Padraic Colum's drover's Eden
I am surrounded by the earthly
and the invisible:
the music of forever swaying the trees,
the prophecies of Old Moore's Almanac
being taken down to read at night.

I am standing in a painter's scene:
the tinge of russet,
winter's glass-clear air. I am listening
to the song that brought me where
green pastures made your Arcadia.

SHANTY

My father's father,
known for his navigator's knowledge of the stars,
was filled with nostalgia
for ropeknots, anchor-chains,
arriving in the harbour from the night-pastures
of the sea. What he loved most
were the lights of the coast,
the seatowns issuing smoke
in wet November.

My father's father
knew the sea for what it was:
a proper bastard smirking in the darkness,
filling the fat pockets
of the harbour master.
Rising from his sailor's bed
his sixth sense told him not to trust
the complete stillness of dawns that felt
like the first day of the world.

TWO

SNAPSHOTS
for John F. Deane

One image shows the shards
of Kristallnacht, a boy not sure what
he's running to and running from.

In snapshots taken by history's witness
there is always a spectre
worn into the grain, into the moment:

the camp survivor, the famine nomad.
The skin-and-bone refugee
behind the barbed-wire fence

or the war-child naked on the Asian road:
a ballerina in a ballet of explosions.
One image shows the fires of Dresden,

another, from the torture-chamber,
is of a man whose corpse resembles
Mantegna's Christ.

MESOPOTAMIA

No light tonight from the Star of Peace
only those warplanes carrying new missionaries
from Michigan, Nebraska, New Orleans.

All the maps are showing a desert route.
The Six O'Clock News comes from the grave
of a hushed city; through telescopic sights

the tracer-fire is viridescent: night-visions
of a grainy *son et lumière*.
It is a story as old as Mesopotamia,
Milton's *Dream of a dream, Shadow of a shade*
haunting the hourly bulletin
                                    and the front page.

POSTSCRIPT

The first of March, too soon
for any burst of skylarks,
too late to stop the executioner.
I have it in a photograph
taken with the Kodak,
a scene of sombre euphoria.
It was Monday and the sun was mostly
on one side of the street.
A gun-carriage wheeled
to the dead march of soldiers' feet.

They were bringing home the bones
of Roger Casement,
postscript to a nation's history.
For this last journey
he travelled slowly and travelled the length
of streets crowded with citizens
of the municipal landscape.
I stood among those assembled
for the quiet conclave of farewells:
women untangling rosary-knots,
broad-shouldered men,
heads bowed, arms crossed
in a gesture of devout concentration.

HAIL AND FAREWELL

Long after Oswald and Ruby
and the photo-opportunity in the ruins of the sun
the face of the dead president was still around,
smiling down on us.
A blissful countenance in the gallery of idols.

They built him a shrine
that was filled with the sound of America weeping.
Some saw him lifted to heaven.
Some sensed his presence pressed to the glass
of their TV screens.

He was the one who beguiled us,
who stood like Harlequin in the open limousine,
in transit between hail and farewell.

THEIR HEMS TOUCHING THE GROUND

Young soldiers at sentry points
let us pass into the one-star town
with three ways of life.

Between souvenirs of Palestine
and psalms of the old religion
we are led to the cradle, the nativity crypt,
back to the beginning,
past the beggars, the war cripples.

There are no bringers
of frankincense or myrrh,
no lifting of hosannas into the air.

In Manger Square,
through the babble of Bethlehem,
the fervour of the crowd,
the people from the Beatitudes move,
their hems touching the ground.

BROTHER OF WATER AND SKY

We came to hear vespers
in a Northern latitude:
the great choir climbing the octaves,
to see quadrangles and clocks,
and night-clouds flying
like Elijah's chariot.

The day is never over,
the night never dark,
not even the hour when all bridges rise
to let the river pageant pass,
the flotilla of tugboat, battleship, barge.
The Baltic amber is honeyed

and opulent. Every noise
is the noise of the past
drumming on the gilded palaces,
St Isaac's and The Admiralty
Tower that Mandelstam described
as *brother of water and sky.*

Anna's Sanctuary

We find it through a hidden entrance:
the arboreal courtyard, Anna's sanctuary
of little rooms that still exhale
the atmosphere of Russia in the age
of forbidden truth.

In this, her church of premonitions,
the ink on her petitions
fades; a shrine is made
of the icon in the icon-corner,
the empty samovar.

And there in Napplebaum's
haunted image Cassandra lives.
Poet with the inward look of the savant,
the look she gives is stoic, chiselled,
black-rimmed beneath a Cleopatra fringe.

St. Petersburg, June 2003

In the War Memorial Museum

In the war memorial museum
a morsel of bread is the centrepiece,
the ration preserved
in the cabinet of blessèd memories.

Watching the blurred documentary
I envisage a scene like Thebes
or Thermopylae or one of those etchings
of imminence from Goya's
Disasters of War.

But first we notice the metronome
steady and constant as a constant vigil.
It is like the heart-monitor
sending its signal, keeping faint hope alive.

The doomsday book is open
at a page inscribed in *bas-relief.*
There's a violin that's shabby
and broken, with the fingerprints
of Shostakovitch.

ELYSIAN COLOURS
(after Tarkovsky's Andrei Rublev)

The horseman on the Asian steed
appears like an evangelist.
Snow falling in a church
leaves a snow-white crust
on the shoulders of Andrei Rublev
stern in his cowl.

The Holy Fool wants to be a wife.
The great bell emits clangourous chimes
over the town of Vladimir.

The strangeness of it all: fires
in a frozen landscape,
the carnal jousts of St John's Night.

The conversation with Theophanes
who called him to his side,
who taught him how to trace the first outline
and paint with Elysian colours
the Byzantine Christ.

GEOGRAPHER'S LANDSCAPE
In memory of Dick Walsh

I think of you as the man who followed the Danube
as far as the house of Elias Canetti.
A mystical quest that brought me once
to a city of bridges where women in headscarves
moved like a tribe, keening
and shaking their wrist-bracelets.

In the opera house I tasted Hungarian wine,
woodwind came alive
during something by Bartók or Haydn.
In the central station I noticed
the allegorical formation of trains that were facing
the east and the west.

The piper's lament
you heard in Milltown Malbay was as ponderous
and melancholy as any Romanian rhapsody.
Yes, I think of you as the man
who followed the Danube: a journey of crossings
through the geographer's landscape.

VILLA FLORICA

In the villa that evening
the birds in the ivy were full of *bonhomie*,
up in the minstrel gallery
warbling their benedictions,
whistling their hearts out.

In the dead heat the thunder shifted
from far beyond to close behind.
Enclosed by trees of great height
we were listening, attentive
to the poet from Lesbos

and the poet who intoned his Balkan elegy
for a homeland that had altered shape.
In the mansion they gave us
a place at the table:
the wine was served from cool carafes,

after that the soup and then the salad
of cucumber and tomatoes.
The dictator's name could not be mentioned
without a chill to break the enchantment,
a theatrical stir in the sylvan camouflage.

SUNDAY MORNING IN ROMANIA

Beware of the dogs, they said.
The ones in packs
that roam the boulevards of Bucharest.
But it is the multitudes on their journey
— between one lost village and the next —
that jam the roads and turn them
into something carnivalesque.

A team of horses stops the traffic,
two of them like sleepwalkers
ambling forth in unison
close to the roadside grass.
Last night's wedding guests have gone
leaving a trace of havoc
in the celebration hall:
ashtrays brimming, bottles drained,
the circle broken where they danced the *hora*
as if to dance was all that mattered.

The silver churches dazzle heaven.
In the Sunday market
there is always one who walks ahead
of everyone else to rummage and haggle
and do the deal with the hawkers selling
craftwork, table-lace, watermelon.

NIGHT IN ST CLOUD
(after Edvard Munch)

The dead come back in dreams:
they knock and enter
the nuptial chamber, the upstairs rooms
where precious things are kept:
Christening robes, glass from Venice.

The dead come back in dreams,
sometimes clearly, sometimes obliquely
like the blurred figure in a family photograph
or the man in shadow
in Edvard Munch's *Night in St Cloud*,

sitting at the window, just as dusk
and fading light alter perceptions in a house
where the mood is indigo
and the pendulum loudens in the lull
after the hours of the day,
the deeds that cannot be undone.

EZRA

Ezra in the ape-enclosure,
a prisoner after the war,
smelling of soap that gives him
the fragrance of Casanova.

Counting his rations by candle-heat:
sugar, horse-meat, a ledger
in which to keep the alphabets
of east and west.

Ezra in the ape-enclosure,
his guard, a crewcut soldier
who does not know
the poet from the felon,

Cathay from Idaho.
Through the eye-hole
in his asylum door he hears Vivaldi
violins, the river-song of Li Po.

HOPKINS

Wearing the blackest black
he arrived with a deep nostalgia
for the music of Henry Purcell.
He arrived by chance like windhover and skylark.

It was a kind of banishment
being sent to that other isle:
tea and bread in the cold Jansenist house,
wet days of summer

in the garrison town beyond the Curragh.
A place to languish,
to listen to horse-traffic
or silence in the noonday chapel.

He arrived from somewhere far,
perhaps where the South Star seemed to hang
or the wind of the valley
was dyed in the Blood of the Lamb.

The Woman who was Bonnard's Wife

Like a dappled Ophelia
she lies in her bath
as a young bride, as the matron
at the end of her life.

His first love, his last love:
the woman who was Bonnard's wife
stands shaded by shutters
or doused in light streaked in to glaze

the salon chairs, the table arranged
for a breakfast of colours.
It never ceased,
the flamboyant, the subdued

courtship of the artist
and the muse whose likeness never aged
but stayed the same
with poise, with insouciance.

EL GRECO

From Alpha to Omega his Greek books
were his books of revelation,
the spirit that moved him,
marked him, made him El Greco.

When he took the road from Toledo
to Madrid, he enjoyed the journey
more than the sojourn: the places of rest,

the towns on the Tagus
that offered bread or where he was guest
of those whose plain sharp faces
appeared again in portraits

of Saint Jerome, emaciated
or Anthony of Padua lost in a trance
like a river-gazing fisherman.

THE PORTUGUESE SINGER

The Portuguese singer stands on stage,
swathed in the cloth she wears,
earthed there, tall and straight.
A swan's-neck straightness.

Her throat-vibrations
rise and fall like fountain water.
She is from Lisbon but resembles
a Pharaoh's daughter.

And when she tells us that next
she'll sing from the song-book
of Fernando Pessoa, I think of a man

obedient to the higher life. A chameleon,
sometimes not sure which world he's in,
which quest he's on

LAST TRUMPET BLOWING

Miles Davis in his mourning suit,
the master of synthesis.
In the monochrome era of jazz
in Club Nocturne
he stands and delivers
a ballad to the most beautiful woman
he's ever seen.

Soloist on his feet,
the last trumpet blowing.
With his glow-in-the-dark cigarette
he leans back in his own sweet rhapsody:
the shimmy of *Autumn Leaves*.

Miles Davis in the years of his bad medicine:
an Orpheus with shoulder-length tresses,
curled fingers dextrous
as they shift in a dance
or build a song of stillness
in unison with the sax.

THE ARTIST AS EULOGIST
(after Sean McSweeney)

The artist paints the ephemeral haze
of a sky in the west, works the spell that makes
the wetland pool a window to the underearth.

The artist as eulogist scans the landscape,
its tones and tints: nimbus, spindrift,
the mountain slope of rock and stone.

Like *those dark trees* that Frost looked on
with worn-out eyes, the trees of Lissadell
are weather-beaten, Venetian red.

The artist needs to fill vast space
with bog-soil, shoreline, a native bloom
that leaves a native stain. The ground is rich,
damp with rain, the last ridge of light
blue as the welder's flame before it glimmers out.

Wonderland
(after Nick Miller)

Snow when it falls is a snowy blanket.
Numinous. Galactic. Like plumage
on the scrawny branches.

It is a good landscape for hide-and-seek
in the cold shadows
of whitethorn and maple.

Power-line and telephone cable
catch the rain and let it fall on gorged-on acres,
borderland, forsaken territory.

In this high country roads twist north
into mountains,
into the corona of dense cloud.

The trees work up a chant of incantation
and sing to the lakes:
Lough Arrow and Lough Gill.

The western gale leaves its razor-scrapes.
It is a ragged landscape
of watery illuminations, a wonderland
for the fisherman with patience.

CORRIB

The day we sailed the Corrib
the lough behaved like a cosmic force,
capricious and primordial.

Our vessel swayed
like the vessel in the hands
of the potter who shapes the clay.

It all happened as suddenly
as the way we sometimes turn our lives.
With seeing-eyes you took it in:

the river bank appearing
and disappearing and then the lake,
a small expanse compared

to your Great Lakes of Michigan.
You stood on deck in heavy weather.
I stayed below in the circle of story-tellers.

There was no shelter, no anchorage.
No safe passage through thrashing spray
to Annaghdown,

the day we sailed the Corrib, upstream
to where the land became unseen
like the Land of Promise.

THE HISTORY OF FOG

Nothing bothers the man who observes
the weather in Clew Bay,
the squalls, the lacquered haze.
The quick sketch he makes
is of seacliff, rockface, sky so low it touches
the turf-meadow, the white gables.

They live on a faultline.
The people who know the history of fog,
whose tracks remain under the reek
and close to the *duach*.
Sea-hunters, bog-cutters,
those who lit the beacon for the lost

armada of musket men.
In the country of apparitions
a little gust becomes a gale
commodious enough to lift up
and carry away the Céide Fields
and famine village harboured in the glen

PAPERWEIGHT

The stone I use as a paperweight
was found on a seashore in Mayo,
summers ago when we drove on the coast
and came to a cove not named on the map
of the Four Provinces.

The stone has been with me since.
It is the size of a fist, hard as a kernel,
lethal enough for Cain to kill Abel.
An ocean gift to the Connaught wind,
it was shaped by many weathers
and worn down by millennia
like the mountain in Mayo that listens to prayers
and disappears sometimes into the rain.

CROSS OF MOONE

What startled us was the rattle of gridiron,
the gravel track twisting under the tyres.
We were driving east, clocking the distance.

Oozing in the heat of late afternoon
the black tar was viscous
on the motorway of our Iliad.

We were driving east but stopped off
at the Cross of Moone, symbol of the creed
of fatherland and mother-tongue.

It was one of the first of the last days of summer.
The tops of conifers brightened and dimmed
and filled with birds with only one song.

Song of innocence, prayer without words.
It was not the beginning and not the end
but the in-between time before Amen

ON THE TRAIN WITH JUDY GARLAND

We are leaving the coast,
the seafarer's road to Utopia.
The train sounds weary, it is old stock.
The branch line runs between

dry-stone walls and bushes of gorse.
There are small estuaries,
inlets where the day ends in solitudes
that feel cold and fill with sudden stillness.

We hurtle through provincial stations
and slow down when it's time to stop
for new passengers.
The girl on the seat opposite,

like a young Judy Garland,
has become my three-hour figment
of infatuation. Sometimes she seems
on the verge of speaking

but really she is occupied by what she sees
in nature: the vernal landscape
in the window frame,
the black raincloud like a mascara stain.

DOWNTOWN

There is menace in the air
Of tragedies in the making.
Charles Simic

Downtown in cellars and attics,
in the banking halls and mail-sorters' office
it is black night, a weekend off.

A raw wind kicks the prophylactics
left on the ground.
There is rhythm in the tumult

of our chief estate: the spangled arcades.
The courier with the flask of donor's blood
weaves through the maze

of red lights, green lights,
the plastic shine and city noise
of city streets moving at a pace.

Everyone carries a piece of the news:
what they saw, what they heard
at the scene of the wreckage:

the empty shoes, last words.
The siren hurrying
to the stopped heart, the severed artery.

AMSTERDAM
for Pauline

Smoothing the creases
in an old photograph
I see a face like yours,
a face like mine:
the two of us, nestled close
in leather sandals and light clothes,
stopped on our way
through Amsterdam
where we crossed many bridges
in search of Ann Frank's
timbered attic,
the tempestuous colours of Van Gogh.

There was no room
in those narrow streets
of huckster stalls, narcotic scents.
Bicycle bells made heraldic chimes
between canals
and courtyards bearing the scars of wartime.
In an unremembered place
we stopped to smile
for the street-photographer
whose camera was unpitying
and rendered us as visitants of summer,
two orphans in a fairy-tale

LATE NEWS

I had just put down the book
of Sylvia's torments:
Ariel pinned to the ground
Lady Lazarus kept in her shroud.

I was on the verge of quenching the light
when the late news came on:
a litany of sorrows,
a calm announcement
of hatreds that have no day of rest.

So it goes. And so I switched
to a different station, listened instead
to Marley and the Wailers
being evangelical, resonating
the rhythms, the patois
of Jamaican reggae.

THREE

SYRIA

(after Montale)

Poetry rises like rungs to God,
declared the elders. But maybe not if my verse
is the verse you look at. Through you my voice returned.
This I understood that day when day became unbound,
exploding from the jaggy peaks:
a congregation of goats and clouds swooped down to sweep
away thorn-bush and river-reed, and the meagre visages
of sun and moon were coterminous;
the auto seized and stopped and streaked in blood
an arrow on the rock of ages
pointed towards Aleppo.

GLENDALOUGH

He found his way
to a place of imperturbable serenity,
a garden of roots and tendrils.
Glendalough where he rested
his body on fern and moss.

To ward off temptation
he stepped into the lake
until it rose to his knees, to the rope
around his waist.

It was his portal to God, his place
to stop and hear the wind
passing over the treetops,
carrying the rook and the crow.

Now in early October
in the twenty-first century
Glendalough remains as it always will be:
Kevin's bed, the tower, the cross.

The dead have their vaults,
the wind has its tree
in the garden of roots and tendrils,
fern and moss.

INTERLUDE

Looking at thorn I think
of the thorn-covered God. I sit and listen.
An insect is scratching the wall.
My wristwatch, ticking obstinately,
sends out a sound like a clenched
fist hammering and hammering.

In the yard a bony chicken
is picking at patches of sunlight.
Implements of the fields are going rusty
where the wet weather touched them.

Today we are submerged in the requiem
music of Good Friday.
The tree with its back turned to the house
is tranquil, as if it were dead.
Tomorrow
we'll be at each other's throats again.

SIMULACRUM

The famous statue behind bullet-proof glass
is of two figures made intransient
by Michelangelo. The seated madonna,
the son on her lap a dead weight
weighing her down.

The pallid marble replicates
wrist-bone, shoulder-blade, cumbrous cloak
on which is laid a body that looks
not dead but sleeping.

The woman's expression drained of blood
is one of mother-love or lamentation
over limbs that are broken,
flesh that seems wasted.

The famous statue, Michelangelo's Pietà
stands undiminished, a simulacrum
that has come through the ages.

ENCOUNTER

From nowhere comes the voice
of supplication. Silencing all questions
the smoke of incense hoists a chant
of baleful bygone Latin.

The entry door is varnished wood
and the hanging lamps
flicker in the sanctuary
where the light is light from another world.

Where sunlight collides with chapel glass
a hermit stands in fire
reciting, perhaps, the last of the psalms
or the story of Isaac.

Veronica got there first,
improvising with her veil,
wiping the unbeloved: the face
of the Son whose gaze is gazed upon.

FOUR

A New Tenancy

Above the hall-door, stained-glass lettering
spells *Cranmore*:
the name suggests that long before
the marriage beds and cradles
a tree with bowers stood erect,
rustling where the house was built,
where eaves and attic came to exist.

The history of the house begins
in 1911: an English officer takes possession.
Moustachioed like Wilfred Owen,
he stood amid tasselled-fringes, war medals,
rooms crammed with the assemblage
of domesticity. Everything then
was still radiant, pristine:

brass and brick and balustrades
that split the late sun at evening
as it filtered through skylight glass,
window drapery. Eighty years later,
in the last decade of the century,
we came to peel back layers of paint,
to create a new tenancy.

HOUSEWARMING

For luck we brought a nugget of coal
and salt: the double talisman
to protect our four walls and fire-hearth.
The on-off switch bestowed electric light
that was all yours, all mine, all we had.

We were ankle-deep in builder's rubble,
dwellers of a bare house,
hammering nails and sweeping the dust,
making the space around us feel like home.

Bare wood cracked like knuckle-bone
when we crossed the floors
or climbed the stairs to take our places
side by side in the last sliver of dusk,
the first rays of the sun.

LAST STAR SMOULDERING

It was one of those dawns
at the end of April,
on a road where old farms disappeared
under concrete and cement.
On the high-tension cables
there were pearls of wetness after rain.
An early freshness in the rinsed-out air.

I was coming home to the suburb on the hill:
pasture-land where new families
settled back to back.
The first cough of the morning
could be heard through walls
in the cul-de-sac; then the stutter
of engine noise: a man off to earn his bread.

From the places where they spent
the night, sparrows flew
diminutive and transient.
I was coming home to sanctuary and fortress.
Milk on the doorstep,
the last star smouldering.

AUBADE

Every day I wake
to the moonclouds of the night,
one side of the mountain
— what the artist painted when he looked upon
a faint horizon of kerosene light.

I wake to someone's hour of prayer,
the epiphanies of daybreak:
feathers in the garden from the feline's feast,
a ghostly fog that lifts to reveal
our urban grass, the metallic shine

of a fleet in slow motion.
In the outer world with the sound turned off
rain bleeds through the tree,
the snail leaves its mark:
a silver smear on the red path.

SIBELIUS

This is the moment to listen to Sibelius
and not the wind making a home
in our cherry tree.

The snow glistens
and everything's white at the edges.
A lily-of-the-valley shade of white
covering the nearest places,
making a new earth for the satellite.

It is like the end of the ages.
The sky darkens to pewter grey
and snow keeps falling in a helpless way,
plentiful, earthbound.

It rises from the ground
and stays on the shoulders
of the woman leaving a footprint
and the man who thinks
the snow on his eyelids is the ash of the wind.

OVID IN THE GARDEN

Among the last remnants of leaf-skeletons
let me be Ovid in the garden
waiting for the first green shoots to spring
from ivy on the trellis,
from the tired rhododendron.

Rust on the wrought-iron.
Clothes-pegs clipped to the line.
Dulcet wind-chimes make a pocket noise
that comes in snatches
through bare branches that splinter the light.

The dead garden in its film of frost.
Chalk-white, utterly still.
The best place to bring the tablecloth
and shake from it
the foodcrumbs, the grains of salt.

Let me be Ovid in the garden
waiting for the solstice,
the equinox; the burning bush
to break into blossom,
the summer apples to dangle and fall.

Backyard

I watch the way the first hours creep
into our small backyard.
Dawn chorus: call and answer.
Pale light leaching
into the pattern of our pyracantha.

The Gingko tree rising taller
than the house it shades
bends just a little forward
like a woman carrying water.

There are apples dangling
from next door's branches.
The first to drop lie rotten,
a banquet for the worm and wasp.

In urns of terracotta
the good-for-nothing stalks
stand naked, last remnants
of what was: marigolds,
carnations, forget-me-nots.

LONELINESS

Rain sings a requiem in the knacker's yard.
At the edge of wasteland
a child's plaything is discarded, suddenly
and forever. Instead of smoke
chimneys shed the soul-stifling melancholy
of nights at the end of June.

The clock strikes, its twelve chimes hypnotise.
Over an unfinished game of chess
someone says *Goodnight*. The light
of the apple-blossom is snatched away.
Watchdogs blend with the quiet
behind closed windows.

Everyone's at rest
except the girl sewing garments for a living.
The house of glass glowing in the dark
is the last bus with only a few travellers
going back to where they began.

Poem Beginning with a Line
from Raymond Carver

The days seemed to pass only to return
again. Like a dream in which one thinks,
I've already dreamt that.
Raymond Carver

That line of Carver's
about *the lightning speed of the past*
reminds me it is two months since
I cut the dead branches
and bagged the leaves that came to the door.

Now it is time for fireworks that dance
in the first night sky of January.
The old year ends with the amity
of people in their glad-rags,
an interlude for lovesongs or laments

or the stroke of midnight
when bells, exhilarant,
seem to walk on air and leave behind
their echo for St Brigid's Day, St Valentine's.

A PREVIOUS LIFE

From what sometimes seems
like a previous life, I remember
the stealth with which we said
Good night beneath St Patrick's clock.

When I received your kiss
it was during the matinee in the dark:
the bicycle scene I think,
in *Butch Cassidy and the Sundance Kid*.

Your kiss was then a healing art
after the dance, under the trees
on Clanbrassil Street,
the corner where in an ardent

trance we drew close
and I placed in your hands
the gospel of Pablo Neruda:
His twenty love poems and song of despair.

EPITHALAMIUM

The night we missed the moon-eclipse
it was late when we stopped
talking about thirty years of marriage:
what we stored up and kept
and what we sometimes let slip through our hands.

How, on the appointed day
you arrived carrying the bouquet
of flowers from paradise,
and I stood waiting in rented suit,
close to where, under the carillon-fugue,

the motley chimes,
Strongbow lies, coffined in stone.
Aoife beside him: child-bride,
chieftain's daughter.
Their marriage a transaction between tribes.